My Wings Battered But I Still Can Fly…

LaMiracle Sims

BookLeaf Publishing

India | USA | UK

My Wings Battered But I Still Can Fly… ©
2024 LaMiracle Sims

All rights reserved.

No part of this publication may be
reproduced, stored in a retrieval system, or
transmitted, in any form or by any means,
electronic, mechanical, photocopying,
recording or otherwise, without the prior
written permission of the presenters.

LaMiracle Sims asserts the moral right to
be identified as author of this work.

Presentation by *BookLeaf Publishing*

Web: www.bookleafpub.com

E-mail: info@bookleafpub.com

ISBN: 9789358319385

First edition 2024

DEDICATION

This book is dedicated to those on the journey of self discovery, self forgiveness, self love, self respect, self care, self embodiment, and self happiness. You are worthy and you are not what you have gone or grown through.

PREFACE

I speak from experience which forms wisdom. I'm gonna let my inner child and my heart speak. Maybe your inner child feels the same way, too. Unleash him or her and just flow. This is a safe haven, leave your armor at the door.

PURPOSE

I was chosen, this wasn't given
According to the world, it's called sinnin'
Accepting that fate, all while grinnin'
Who put you in charge of my destiny?
Perpetrating the truth all in my face.
Making me lose focus, so we could relate.
All dismantled and dark from your trauma,
I'm empathetic, now your trauma my trauma,
This what you wanted though…
To see the calling on my life and my light
blow like a fuse,
Rather than allow my light to ignite the light in
you.
Wait, I'm confused?
This what that thang' called purpose do?
Make you feel all the blues.
Battered and bruised, have you losing your mind
like scattered screws.
That's what they say anyways,
Call me crazy and delusional for saying all the
crazy thangs'.
The crazy thangs' everybody else think but
scared to say.
I know things, which is why I'm labeled crazy
too…

The things that can't be proved,
The things I see in my dreams and profuse from
the third eye in the middle of my medull…(a).
But what can I say?
Many are called but few are chosen,
This life not always golden,
But I'm holding on, cause I'm living in my….
Purpose.

I Know It's My Job But…

I know you been through a lot,
I can see it in your soul,
Let me do my job,
Let me heal your pain,
Starting with your soul.
I know hurt because I've been hurt,
Still hurt at that.
But I care more about caressing the voids within
you,
No matter if you send em' back.
I want you to see and love me,
Even if that means not loving myself.
I know my healing spirit was meant to love on
you,
Forget everyone and everything else.
Even if I have to overextend myself,
Lose sleep and weep,
Wondering how much more I gotta do,
So you can see.
I have your best interest,
I want you to be whole.
But you're too busy going after everything and
everyone else,
That placed you in this hole.
You appreciate and love me back in private,

But in public it's like the love is dying.
No matter platonic, familiar, or romantic,
It's all the same.
I know healing is my job but at this point,
I care more about being sane.

Let Me Out Of Here

What's going on?
I can't quite breathe!
Am I dying soon from the things I don't
achieve?
What does it take to be a great?
Do I have to always keep myself dressed up,
Get degrees with a high paying job,
Or even go overseas?
What does it take?
Am I not good enough in my natural state?
I spend so much time, in my mind,
Being pressured by my external world,
When they don't give a dime.
For what though?
Where did this start,
I ask the little girl inside of me,
Who ruptured her heart?
Who told you, you had to be perfect,
To be accepted?
Who made you feel like you had to work hard,
for the very things you were already equipped
with.
Robbed of your innocence,
Turned imposter,
It's okay now baby girl,

We can heal together,
Sipping kool aid over pasta.
No more killing yourself softly,
Like the song said,
The true you still alive,
Let's be her, instead…

Beast

You can't tame me, I'm a beast.
Whatever obstacle you place in my way,
I will most certainly defeat,
Cause I'm a beast.
I'm the one, you have to try and tame.
I'm the one, you know my name.
But do you really know the story behind this
pain?
Do you know, you see the glory, but not this
pain?
They always say the rose that grew from
concrete,
I say what about the beast inside of me.
The beast in me can slave the pavement,
The beast in me can heal an ailment.
The beast in me can save the day.
The beast in me that has to have it its way.
The beast in me that can make the day go night.
The beast in me that make your shadows seem
bright.
The beast in me that preserves its fight.
The beast in me that causes fright.
Or… the beast in me that can make you go
goodnight.
Through it all, we both stood tall.

All in all, we did the ball.
All in all, we won at ball.
All in all, we accomplished it all.
Now what about the rest of the calls….

Twin Flame

Break down my walls.
You do that, when you show me where it hurt.
You mirror my pain and it's tough,
When you tell me all the wrong but right stuff.
I'm so used to the bluff, but you call me out on
my bluff,
You show me I'm tough but not so rough.
How I'm still feminine and don't have to operate
out my masculinity.
I don't have to keep the barriers up,
I can leave them where I stand.
You open me up to me,
Like no one else ever can.
How do you do that?
You make me feel so safe and vulnerable
At the same time and in the same rhyme,
You make me stumble over my words,
Cause I never wanna run out of time,
Talking to… you.
You always know what to say.
You really get me, do you study me?
Cause I swear it's like you know everythang'.
From what makes me mad, to what makes me
sad,

To what makes me whole, to caressing my
soul… to my shoulders.
When you do that, the feelings grow more
immense and bolder.
I swear I met you in another life,
When I was your wife.
Where it didn't matter the price,
As long as the time we spent was priceless,
Like a rollie on ice.
But now it's different,
You showing me where it all went wrong,
And exactly how I can fix it.
Where I can feel it and where I can heal it.
You bringing me closer to who I really am.
Yes, I can feel it…..
Thank you.

Moment Of Silence

Shhhh. Moment of silence.
My innerg is talking.
Shhhh. Moment of silence.
My energy has spoken.
I'm peepin' you, I'm seein' you,
They wonder how cause you ain't even talkin'.
It's that thang in me.
That thang that swang,
Like a pendulum letting me know, you danger
and you not ok.
Moment of silence…
Let's make it real quiet.
Let me decipher between the hyper vigilance
I've adopted,
And between that inner thang in me.
Let me decipher between,
What I'm being told but what's been really seen.
Moment of silence.
When it gets quiet, just know.
I'm far from foolish and sometimes,
I wish I just didn't know.
Moment of silence.
My grace, my kindness.
Don't be blinded.
Even if I don't say nothing,

While I'm in my silence.
Even if I don't say nothing,
And keeping silent.
Just know I know,
Especially during moments of silence.

You Get Me

Finally! Someone that sees me.
Finally! Someone that believes me.
No more fighting, the dark red fight.
No more being viscous, angry, crying each
night.
I don't have to work so hard any more.
I don't have to be or do more than my beautiful
soul already implore.
Easy like a breeze, on a cool summer night.
You light up my world, and restored the life in
my light.
Went from being blue to giving hue,
You poured in me and I was able to subdue.
I always did the pouring, I always did the
scoring,
Now I don't have to be so selfless anymore,
You taught me how to spread my own wings,
Go out in the world,
And soar.
You taught me how to love me and put me first,
You taught me that being selfish wasn't a bad
thing,
It was a right of mine since birth.
You taught me how to listen to my body,
Over anybody,

Cause they'll lead me astray.
You taught me how to channel that inner thing,
And listen to all it had to say.
You taught me how to eat my way to health, and
eat to dodge death.
You taught me how to feel my surroundings,
And stop sharing my sacred energy,
Just to say I was there,
Because I was so powerful,
It didn't matter where I was,
Present or not, I am always felt.
You taught me I was different, in a good way,
I made a difference, more than anythang.
You taught me I was her and that's why they
tried to make me think I wasn't.
You taught me I was able to do it all,
And losing me was the biggest fumble.
For anyone else and even for myself,
You taught me I was everything the world
needed,
It's me above all else.
Because if I'm not the best me for me,
I can't be the best me for anyone or anything…
Else.

Love Letter

This love letter is to myself,
For all the times I let you down.
For all the times I wanted to speak up,
But was afraid to speak a sound.
I'm sorry for not listening to how you felt.
I'm sorry for putting others before you,
No matter how it made you feel.
I'm sorry for always telling you "later",
But for them I would jump in a hurry, without a
worry.
I apologize for putting you through so much
pain.
I apologize for being so hard on you,
Letting you feel all this shame.
I apologize for being in you but not for you.
I apologize for letting you get empty.
I apologize for not showing and giving you love,
when I had plenty.

Here I Am

Here I am. Starting from scratch,
Don't know which way to go, which road to
take, but consider it done.
It's lonely even while being surrounded by
plenty,
They all told me they loved me but as I look
around, it ain't many…
left.
Left like me, the last on the shelf.
They saw me as a meal ticket, while leaving me
starving,
Starving to know how to live and not just
survive,
The emotions it all left me with,
Just suppressed and continuously thrive.
How could you? How could you!
You left me for dead. You played with my head.
You left me on my death bed…
Here I am, trying to figure this out.
You acted like you were really with me,
Tell me what this really was about.
I dig deep inside cause I know I'm equipped,
Equipped for every flip, dip, and trip.
You did me some damage, but that wasn't
enough.

I lift my head to the skies above,
And they help me get it done.

I Can't See… But I Can Fly.

Yes, I can see. I can see perfectly fine.
I have never had to visit an optometrist at that.
When I stated I could not see, as you read in the title, it correlated to something totally different. The tears. The tears of worry. The tears of fear. The tears of hopelessness. The tears of desperation. The tears of unbalance. The tears that clogged my eyes. The steam that filled my forehead. Through these malicious things, I could still fly. Though life is a blur at times, I still soar. Who could steal my fate? What could destroy my purpose? Only me, that is who. So, as I cry...I still fly. As I hurt, I still fly. As I wonder why, I still fly. As I sleep, I still fly. Now what would happen if I stopped because my cries. If I stopped because I cried, there would be nothing to cry about in the first place. Reform, possibilities, open doors, and answers await me. I must find out. Every one of those things will not always result in the best. I may become crushed when it does not result in great matters but that will not halt me from pressing forward. I can't see...but I can fly.

Skin

I'm shedding like a butterfly leaving its cocoon
skin.
It hurts to shed the skin, the dead weight, the
dual…
Facing the person in the mirror versus the person
in my soul,
I see the goal, help me hold on.
I'm growing and it hurt so bad,
The good hurt, though.
The kind that brings success,
Happiness, and peace that ever lasts.
God, my spirit Gods, and my ancestors,
Hold my hand.
Hold my hand, as I shed this dead skin.
Hold my hand, as you all collectively set me up
to win.
Hold my hand, as my face hit the wind.
The wind that tries to cause turbulence,
From seeing who I am again.

She's A Runner, She's A...

My confession is that, I like to run.
Not to have fun but just to run.
Run from place to place,
To different states,
To different tastes,
To different people,
To different foods,
To different cars,
To different schools.
Who are you trying to fool?
To look this good.
To be this hood.
To be this intelligent.
But yet still so misunderstood.
Where you running?
Are you even running?
Or are you still in place,
Just taking up space.
Wishing you were in space,
Rather than be in the place….(s)
You despise,
Or around the people that demise.
Or around the things that's a waste of time.
Or around, just existing, not collecting a dime.
Or, just in your mind.

Who are you running from?
Are you even running?
Or are you afraid of facing the one,
The one that can put you on top,
And also the one that can pull the gun.
And the one, that call the shots,
the one that say it ain't over til I say it's done.
Or the one, that can cry in a second, then next
say it's over, she good, she done.
Or the one, that can kill em' with looks alone.
Or the one, that can fail right now and still get it
done.
Who you running from?
What you running from?
Are you even running?
Or are you not answering the call…
Standing tall, in the purpose,
Most powerful of them all.
You running from yourself,
You don't need help,
You not crazy,
You just lazy,
You scared to be great,
Cause great is your fate.
You scared to fail,
Cause they might tell.
But listen, who cares.
You her.
Don't you ever forget.

You not running,
you fooling yourself,
The more you try to run,
The harder it get.

Umbilical Cord

Deny you, how could I do?
You are me and I am you.
Did it for many years,
Didn't understand the things I feel.
I was ashamed of your name,
I was so angry on the inside,
And you the one I blamed.
That was not right,
I'm sorry it was me that stood in fright.
I'm sorry I was another one of the reasons,
You cried at night.
I didn't understand then,
But now I do.
Nobody tried to understand that you were
human, too.
Nobody tried to understand that you were
fighting internal battles,
Leaving you aloof.
I could only imagine how tough it must've been,
Living a life without the lives you gave and
everyone else just pretend,
That you didn't exist, sort of like I did, for some
time.
I now know it was wrong but please forgive me
now.

I'm thankful that you said YES to me.
Just for that, the best I'll be.
Although not here physically,
Your spirit reign now vigorously.
Our story filled with ups and falls,
God still promises me this is not all.

Wraith

The anger inside of me,
It burns like a blaze.
Having to suppress my emotions,
For so many years,
Put me in a rage.
Showing up as someone I'm not,
Just to make you feel comfortable,
Well now that's over, the real me gone make the
world rumble like a jungle.
You could've gotten to know the real me,
Rather than trying to see how much you could
change.
You thought you knew who I was,
Whole time you just knew my name.
I'm a victor, not a victim
Regardless of the cards dealt.
My energy inevitably strong,
Like a wraith, it will be felt.

Hood Healer

Can I soothe you in all the right places,
Touch your mind in spaces that it's never seen,
Laying out in evergreens,
Evergreen trees or blowing green.
Whatever that may mean… ha.
No drugs involved,
My loving standing tall,
Making you feel immaculate,
Above all.
Don't you feel it? How it get to you.
Fill the voids and crevices,
Like no one else could ever do.
Yearning for my love,
Earning for your trust.
Filling you up, cause you on E,
This love super, premium, like 93.
I love making the hairs on your neck stand,
You can't get enough of me,
Wanting time to slow down like quick sand.
You feel me, without feeling me,
Within me without digging deep,
My words alone could make your day,
Hear my voice and shake away.
Mmm, from tasting pain to making love in rain,
You know I like em a lil hood right,

Just left Johnny D, with the gold grillz tight,
Say my name,
Like whatcha name.
Can I make you feel like,
A box chevy on gold rims like?
Or a Monte Carlo on big rims like?
Or even a caprice with the missing top piece?
You know this loving deep,
Have you all in the trap feeling trapped,
Thinking you loss the best thing since Baps.
I ain't going no where tho'.
This that type of love yo type kill fo'.
This that type of love yo type heal from.

Alone

I just be wanting to be by myself sometimes.
Really all the time, I just make time.
I feel my best when my energy not being tested.
My energy is pure when it's not being projected.
My energy is pure when it's being protected.
I feel good alone.
I don't have to feel and see everything and
everyone like a drone.
I feel good alone.
I don't have to dim my light to make you feel
less dethroned.
I feel good alone.
I feel good at home.
I feel good in me.
I feel good at peace.
I feel good at me.
I love being alone.
I love my energy and power to myself.
Selfish, for no one else.
No one else but myself,
I've given it as enough help.
More peace and power in myself.
It's you that need my help.
But now I must help myself.
It's me that need my help.

I'm gone take the steps.
I must replenish myself.
I just need to be alone.

Me

Heal me.
See me thru.
See me through.
See through me.
Get me.
Feel me.
Listen to me.
Feed me.
Hug me.
Love me.
Respect me.
Sustain loyalty.
Pour into me.
Ground me.
Surround me.
Unbound me.
Let me be me.

I Won, I'm One.

When they told me I couldn't do it,
I did it 20 times.
It's just something about hearing the doubt,
Eating it up, spitting it out!
Doing the work, then later on hearing them clap.
I wish I knew it was that easy,
for people to be for me this week,
Then next week try to tease me…
For being human.
Soon as you up, everybody around
When you down, nobody around.
But, everything you did was for them right?
Listen to how that sound, this can't be real right?
It was then, I really decided to win,
To win within,
what I should have done to begin.
Because you can show up for the world
And they'll turn around and pretend… like,
Just last night everything wasn't alright,
And act like tonight, one simple fright,
Just turned it all off, like the kitchen light.
My biggest advice is to just be yourself,
For yourself,
Don't listen to nobody else,
Do everything for you, nobody else.

Haus Of Me.

If I let you in my place.
Let you in my space.
You must have a sweet taste.
Cause' not everybody can afford to be in my
space.
Not everybody can afford to be in my place.
When everybody been wanting a taste.
A taste, so they chase.
And chase to inflict my power in hopes of taking
my place.
Persuade me my sacredness need to chase, in
order to be in a place.
When the whole time I've been the chase.
The one that needed space.
The one that needed to protect her place.
The one whose energy so fluid and fluent it can
cause a case.
My space.
My place.
If I let you in my sacred place.
Your spirit must be so pure.
I grew up putting my trust into too many
energies that wasn't so pure.
Nobody know the walls I was up against but just
had to endure.

Nobody knew how many battles I was battling
while battling the biggest battle.
The biggest battle of having to straddle between
choosing them or choosing me,
To believe.
The biggest battle of having to straddle between
honoring you or honoring me.
The biggest battle of having to straddle between
who I am and what I mean.
The biggest battle of having to straddle between
trusting you or trusting me.
The biggest battle of having to straddle between
loving you or loving me.
The biggest battle of having to straddle between
you being queen or me being king..
Only the real ones understand.
It was never to be this way but it was all
planned.
Now I do the planning with no need of an
understanding.
So, if I let you in my place.
Let you in my space.
It's a purpose behind it.
It's resources behind it.
It's enforcement behind it.
Everybody can't come in my place.
Everybody can't come in my space.
Everybody can't be in my face.
Cause now if you come in my space.

Trying to cause confusion and misplace.
It may end in a cold case.
Cause I forgot but you should never forget.
This place got many doors.
Many floors.
And I can cause you to lose it all,
If you enter the wrong door.
Take the wrong floor.
But I been sparing you.
Don't make her do what you know she can do.
Don't make her lace you up like an untied shoe.
Don't make her have to do what she normally
would do.
This my space.
This my place.
Stay out my face.
If you can't face…
Me.

I Know…

My presence is a present.
The greatest gift to God's green earth.
It took me some time to get where I am now.
I refuse to lose, so if you misuse me, you lose
me.
I know my power.
I know my strengths.
I know my weaknesses are still my strengths.
I know I bring life to dead situations.
Dead things.
Dead people.
You alive but you dead on the inside.
I know there's healing power at the edges of my
fingertips,
that's why you so infatuated with me now.
I know that if I let you inside my body, let you
touch my body, every ache you feel and ever felt
goes away.
I know if I open my mouth and speak,
My wisdom and ancient knowledge exposes
everything.
I know I make life worth living.
I know I make life worth feeling.
So, all I have to say, is.
If you come my way,

You need to be able to reciprocate the same.
No more playing games.
No more accepting the chump change.
Because, I'm all that plus tax.
It took me a while to understand the god in me
but I'm never going back.
No more being top shelf accepting small shack.
I know who I am.
I'm not afraid of her anymore.
If that means leaving you behind, so I can soar,
then you hit the door.
I care about me more.
I know who I am.

In The End… Affirmations

In the end…
Way farther than it begin.
It ain't raining no more.
The sun shining on down.
I'm living in my angelic divinity now.
Blue deep ocean gazing from my balcony door.
Hearing chatter, while laughing at my husband
and children scoring on the indoor court.
We made it.
It all worked out.
From feeling pain and being drained,
To being a fruitful mommy now.
I nurture them through nature,
Cause it's my human nature.
I go to sleep and still don't miss out on no paper.
I generate money in my sleep.
I'm a multimillionaire entrepreneur,
fashionista, and artist in the makeup industry.
I get it now.
From being down, feeling like a clown, to being
the biggest in town.
I get it now.
My purpose wasn't to hurt me.
I bustled and tussled with what was my true
divine purpose.

Your calling can crush you,
Until you walk in your truth.
It took me a long time to get here,
But I've helped me so I can help you.
I'm at peace, I can sleep.
I got the funds, we can eat.
No more hiding behind no screen.
I'm really living what I always dreamed.
I stopped doing it for you and did it for me.
Now I'm all over tv.

www.ingramcontent.com/pod-product-compliance
Lightning Source LLC
LaVergne TN
LVHW010828200726

843508LV00012B/2527